TURNING LOSERS INTO WINNERS

IN THE STOCK MARKET

YUL SPENCER

CONTENTS

JOIN THE THOUSANDAIRE
MOVEMENT

Thousandaire members get unique items and are always the first to hear about Yul Spencer's new books, publications and public appearances.

See the back of the book for details on how to sign up.

⚠ WARNING
THIS BOOK ISN'T FOR
PEOPLE WHO THINK
THEY'RE SMARTER THAN
OTHER PEOPLE

INTRODUCTION

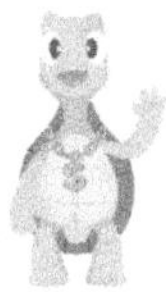

LET ME RE-INTRODUCE MYSELF! I'm Yul Spencer, but you can call me Spencer; those who know me as a professional stand-up comic call me Spencer. Especially the other comics. Should I list a few of them for fun? Naw. I could name many impressive names that I came up with in the comedy world but that's for a different kind of book. But I'm in the class of '88 at the Comedy Store, Improv and the Laugh Factory. As an actor, I'm credited as Yul Spencer; my mother named me Yul, which made it easier for the police to find me. I was the only Yul in the hood, believe me. I found out a few years ago that "Yule" means Christmas in the Netherlands. They have a Yule log celebration every year and turns out I used to do a lot of Christmas shows. #NoMistakes

I was labeled the Christmas comic by some comedy bookers. I bring gifts in jokes, and I receive gifts like a newborn in a manger. The audiences bring incense, money, and gold. I'm fu**ing wit' ya, but I'm also serious. I don't ask them to do it. They "just do it" like Nike.

Anyhow, I'm back with the second book of the *Wall Street-Smarts* series. Let's stay focused on stacking racks. I'm going mainstream with these books, adding some comedy will just be a natural thing for me to do. I hope you have a great sense of humor coupled with a desire to improve your finances. The stock market has never been this funny to anyone. "You'll run out of money before I run out of funny." #EG www.yulspencer.com

However, I believe brevity is the best way to deliver new information to new traders and investors. No one seems to have the time to sit down to read a 277-page book on trading and investing (or any other subject) these days. *War and Peace* forget 'bout it! #Ebook

Our time is precious, so this series has been written in bites so that it's easier to digest page by page, book by book and audio books too. We're going to cover in more detail in this book most of the things I shared with you in my first book, *Wall Street Smarts*. In this book, we'll discuss market dynamics, risk management, entering trades, and how to exit trades as well.

Each of the books in this series will inch you closer to becoming more and more encouraged to get in the game and become a CPT (consistently profitable trader). "Inch by inch, it's a cinch." #ZigZiglar

The $400 financial crisis isn't over yet, and I plan on writing until it has been proven to me that more of you have begun your own funds for fun, and now it's a business for you. Once I start entering gatherings and having strangers come up to me not for a photo or an autograph but to tell me they have more than $400 in their pockets and can spend it on whatever they like. Maybe even me. When that happens, my heart will be filled with appreciation. It'll be a #HappyDay for me. Maybe then I can slow my roll in writing these books for Americans who are still unaware that the stock market is a legal and viable way in today's "technological apocalypse" to get that money you need for extra sh**. To turn a lil' money into a lot of it.

Allow me to be repetitious here, some readers who used to trade and invest back in the day got blown out because they didn't really understand the game or never figured out that it *is* a game and that they didn't possess any "game" themselves to start with. So they got played, and now all they know how to do is "save" a bunch of cash (by owning a home, boat, jewelry, etc). And now that cash doesn't go to work for them anymore; it just sits in a bank paying them nothing. (*Wall Street Smarts*)

The 2008 market crash has financially handicapped citizens so badly that they're looking for parking spaces that weren't created for them. Some have actually applied for the handicap sticker to no avail. The American people of that time had been literally frightened out of the market to never return to it. This reaction to the market has been like no other crash in history. (Crashes are a thing in the stock market, actually. We're overdue for one soon.) #2020

If you live in California, you'll get this, and if you don't, you'll get it anyway because you have your own climate disasters to look forward to every year. I've been in most of the earthquakes here in LA. I've been here since 1988 so I have some real experience in surviving them.

But waiting for each crash in the stock market is like sitting around waiting for and trying to predict the next earthquake. We don't know when that will be. Some of us are prepared, but most of us aren't I'm guessing. Because most of us aren't living our lives thinking about when it's going to happen. It's like dying. No one wants to talk about it because that sh** could happen at any time, and most folks like to ignore the worst about living. So, the earthquake comes. BOOM, ah sh**, we're going down, but it's over in like forty-five seconds. And most of us are fine if we can hold on between a doorway or under a mattress and wait for the ground to stop shaking except for a few aftershocks. Then we clean up all that was damaged. We mourn the loss of any humans and pets. And then we get back on track and go back to living our lives not worrying about the next earthquake. But those who were frightened by the earthquake left California never to come back, except maybe to visit. And, after visiting, some move back to Cali. #TrueStory

That's how some of you might feel getting back into the stock market if you've been out since 2008. I get it. I say that to be empathetic, but really, I'm not empathetic at all, except for to those who trusted brokers and their firms to manage your money for you, and I do mean ALL of your money. If I could say here that's something to never do again for sure; don't let one firm or one financial advisor manage ALL your money. Wall Street Smarts will tell ya that's a bad idea. If you have that much money, let a firm manage some but not ALL.

#AmericanGreed

You take as much as you can handle and manage it yourself. Every day, it'll be worth it. What amazed me during that crash of 2008 was that if more partic– ipants knew what they were doing back then, they would've stayed in and got PAIIID! (Unless, of course, they were one of the many Americans that let someone else other than themselves manage all their money.) The stock market isn't going anywhere; only people go. Mr. Market will outlive us all.

Nevertheless, it's not easy to understand an event you really don't know anything about. What caused the crash? Who caused it,

and what did it have to do with you personally? The fearful public couldn't see it had nothing to do with them; they were too busy crying about what they believed they thought they lost. It was impossible for them to see through all those tears, because so many were unprepared. Bad risk management. They couldn't see the opportunities the market was giving at the time (and has given since then, for that matter). Instead, the headlines were what came to their attention—they're what "Mainstreet" Americans remember most. #Occupy-WallStreet

The next thing they heard to do was to stay away from the markets. Axel, from the television show *Billions*, and I seem to be the only people I was aware of who weren't afraid to see the opportunities. Too bad Axel is a character on a television show. But I'm not. (Not this week, anyway.) What I'm saying is that I admit, I bought a few stocks during that drop. I was a big consumer of Jamba Juice at the time, loving the Orange Dream Machine. When I saw the stock at under a dollar, I knew from watching its history that it was worth much more than a dollar. So, I bought what I could afford and made a nice grip. This is actually how I caught on to that buying low and selling high thing that's supposed to be dead in the market. Sh**, I find out this is where the big profits are. Not necessarily riding some trend higher than it already is and trusting it to keep going higher, but you can do that if you'd like. The lower the buy, the larger the spread and the higher the sell. #PayMe

Real-life people have been made to fear investing in an economy that they help create and sustain with the money they already earn in wages. The *Wall Street Smarts* series is trying to assist the American public to shift gears and turn those earnings they work so hard for into more money. Why more money? Because everybody seems to need it. No one seems to have enough of it, so these books will lead you to the well of wealth that still exists in this country and others (global markets) and show you how to drink from it.

Why should you be broke? I'm not asking, but it's something you might want to ask yourself. I remember when we used to write personal checks to pay bills. I used to fill them all out for the month of

May... they *may* clear... and they *may* not clear. We'll just have to wait and see. #Joke

I'm not doing that anymore. I'm not avoiding any bills these days, but I don't incur many of them either. If you've already begun turning losers into winners, I congratulate you. You have more "grit" and money than the girl or guy sitting next to you. You can even pass on the knowledge. See, it becomes this huge snowball effect as the snowball rolls down the hill. It gets bigger and bigger (momentum) until it hits up against a tree and spreads everywhere. Putting an end to everyday "broke-ness" is the core mission of every book that will be written in this series. #Boom

MARKET DYNAMICS MATTER

MARKET DYNAMICS MATTER and should be considered before entering into the market or executing any trade to buy or sell. What do I mean by "market dynamics?" Basically, are we in a BEAR market or a BULLISH one. Where in the market cycle are we? I mean that you'll have to know what's going on in the market that day, that week, that month, and even for the last fifty years. Not really but really. It will help you make better decisions. You'll have to be up on current market trends as well as having an array of data about the future. You must understand the stock market as a whole. Is it currently overvalued or undervalued?

. . .

How do the politics of your time play into the movement of the market? What is the current administration up to? Have you heard of the Federal Open Market Committee (FOMC), a.k.a. the Fed? It would certainly behoove you to bookmark their website. Everyone invested in this stock market—including the global markets—hangs onto every word the Fed spews at meetings and press conferences. It's crucial that you keep up with them as an investor. If you're a long-time investor, the Fed doesn't have as much of an effect on you as it does for day traders and speculators. Knowing what the currencies are up to is important. (For me, on a psychological basis, it confirms and represents permanent liquidity in the markets forever.) The stock futures give you a feel for where the world is at. The market is vast and it all comes to you through your computers. There is so much going on every day for the thousandaire investor to keep up with, but you can do it for the most part. You're living it. Being an investor increases your self- awareness. Never worry about what you can't see the market doing; concern yourself with what you can see. There will be too many *invisible intangibles for you to catch or think you know everything, but you can't know everything. So give it up and just know what you can find out to make a positive decision.* One warning about money: money never sleeps, only humans do. #Forex

Those of you who only get dreams in their sleep and would rather be up living them really enjoy the "twenty-four-seven" of this business. Actually, every week is an event. It's like being in the playoffs forever. If you're someone who just wants to get the part-time money in this game, it is possible to come off the bench and be profitable. You don't have to be as active as I have described in these pages, but the investors who end up loving this game are hella active. It's not absolutely necessary, though; there is a "slow train" to making more money in the stock market. I've discovered as many personalities in the stock market as there are ways to trade it.

You will learn a bunch of acronyms, ticker symbols, and trading strategies. Indicators and charts are the way many view the market in motion in real time. They can help you determine the dynamics of the market, and you will learn about support and resistance levels.

. . .

Nevertheless, you can learn all about these charts, candlesticks, and strategies, along with how they work, online and in many trading books specifically focused on any of these areas. The SMA, EMA, and CCI, all of these indicators and much more are important to those who drop billions every day in the stock market, pension funds, old lady groups, and the billions in the Roth IRA's. It will serve you well to pick up on as much of it as you are willing to learn.

Then there's the VIX: the sentiment gauge otherwise known as the volatility index.

Traders are watching this all the time and even buying into it, but it gives most of us the highest probabilities of where sentiment stands for the day, the week, and the month. When the VIX is under $15, there's low volatility. When it hits above the $20 area, the volatility increases. The higher it goes, the higher the volatility for that trading session. Volatility is a blessing for a thousandaire. Most of our opportunities will show up in a high-volatile market because the prices fluctuate so much that you can probably pick up some stocks you've been dreaming about owning at a price that will surely be profitable to you. You should only buy when the prices are overwhelmingly in your favor to make a profit. And you'll know it if you've been hunting it down to a price you know you can win. 52-week lows are good for this kind of "snatch & grab." Understand that a part of comprehending the dynamics of the market isn't, in most cases, what you personally think is happening or going to happen but rather what your competitors and the markets think is happening or going to happen. It's those folks on the other side of the trades we sometimes forget about. What do they think?

We must learn to anticipate the movements of the stock of your choice. Not just follow and stalk it. That will usually cause traders to react on fear or greed. Anticipating the movement of a stock will prevent the trouble of trying to predict tops or bottoms of a stock price. Anticipation allows you to plan for what you think is going to happen and then react to that if your anticipated move turns out to be correct.

. . .

For example, the marijuana sector and industry are just beginning to make major moves. You may not be a "pothead"—you may have never even experienced smoking, ingesting, or using any marijuana in any capacity. It's hard to believe these people are out there, but I have met some of them, and let me note they're not the happiest bunch in our population. At the time I'm writing this neither are the early investors and shareholders or GIANTS in the game the MARKET MAKERS have been pushing this sector lower and lower. I suspect all the palms in this industry have not been greased yet. Police, big pharma, government and the like. Now this is only my street-smarts suspicions. I could be wrong. However, you've also been reading about how Big Pharma is going to play a huge role (Pharma being an industry you do comprehend) in the evolution of cannabis and CBD.

Now, because you fill your own prescriptions at the corner pharmacy every week, you strike up a conversation with your pharmacists about the move. You might end up chatting with your kids if you have any (you'd be surprised by how helpful the youth are when you need to learn something about the future). Maybe call up some old friends or relatives that you almost smoked some weed with back in the day before deciding to stick with alcohol, and someone tells you they're about to infuse your favorite alcohols with CBD in the future. So, you may not like or use marijuana, and you might think or feel it has no value to you, but you can see or feel how others do think about it in the market. Then maybe you can find your way to take a trade in this or any other sector of the market that has a pulse and is profitable. Just because you don't agree with or use certain products doesn't mean you shouldn't profit from anticipating the success in any particular industry that you can comprehend (capitalism, baby). It's how this whole thing continues to work and grow. You'll get paid for taking the ride with them. You did start trading to be profitable, correct? It should be somewhere on the top of your list of objectives.

So, I say, google all these many facets of the market and study everything you can get your mitts on, over and over. "Wash, rinse, repeat" is a saying that is used to describe the most basic strategy of trading (if you can call it a strategy at all; it's more of a simplistic action pattern we traders do over and over). And it's one of the reasons why losing stocks can become winners. Because market dynamics do matter before entering a trade. #Anticipation

RISK ALLOCATION AND MONEY MANAGEMENT
(RAMM)

NOW, here's where we separate the boys and girls from the men and women. How well do you really know yourself? How much risk can you stomach? Risk allocation is a serious business. As I've explained, on the real streets, it's taken to a *whole 'nother level.* I've known gangstas who would kill ya for nothing, street kids who would rob you for less than five dollars.

Money is such an emotional thing to humans  because it's attached to everything, we need to be comfortable on the planet. Except, of course, for the planet itself; we kind of need it first, but human beings are so caught up in trying to make it day to day that their focus is on how to get that money. The planet will have to wait ...but can it? I guess that's a topic for another day.

Money is really a driving force in all of our lives. It's why I feel so deeply compelled to keep writing this "joint." Risk, risk, risk; how much do you think you can take and still go about your day without thinking about it? One hundred dollars? Two hundred? Three hundred or a thousand? How much money can you put on a trade without having your stomach turn all day? That amount would be your "risk threshold." If you can't walk away from your investment or trade and take a nap, go for a run, or head back to work without your head spinning all day about what would happen if you lost that amount of money, you have taken on too large of a position. You need to decrease it or get out of it immediately. You're doing too much. #ThatPart (That's what my daughter says to me in reply to most things—or at least when she's agreeing with me—"that part, Dad." She's hilarious.)

· · ·

Listen up! Peep game, Wall Street game, anyone can buy a "stock," that's easy. What improves your probabilities of profit is what you paid for it. The most important criteria are not buying a stock but what you paid for that stock. It's so weird: most participants buy stocks way at the top, then sell 'em when they go down. That's ass backwards. You should prepare to do the opposite if you want to be a profitable trader, and I know you do because you got this book in your hands.

Now, for me, remember I had put together $1,500.00 to work with at the beginning, so immediately I took a third of that and set it to the side, because I didn't want to lose the entire nut. So, I'm working with just a grand now, but I have a nickel put to the side in case I need it for personal use or to buy more of a winning position. If you're peeping game, you have noticed I now have more than an extra $400 to my name. It's that easy, but it's just the beginning. We want more extra cash, don't we? And in order to keep a cash balance of your liking stable and intact you'll have to invest to keep the money making you more money. That's how it's done folks and for some reason it's not easily explained to the masses who don't have any money. That under-standing of how money has to circulate in order to maintain a balance is reserved for only rich folks or institutions with major cash like banks, credit unions and hedge funds. But never you the average citizen who finds it difficult in the richest country in the world to keep four hundred dollars in a savings account. Why? Rich folk money and anyone who plans on staying rich or getting rich knows that money has to go IN & OUT.

Well, I have a lil' news for my readers in order for whatever amount of money you want to stack or keep in your possession it will have to go IN & OUT also. Instead of the only direction the rich would prefer "main streets" money to go...out and spent on their goods and services that they so kindly produce for the consumers consumption! And "these" days it would be in your favor to peep game. To check it out. Otherwise you'll have to invent something or start a company and that can be a long haul. I say it's easier to profit with companies that are already in place and profiting. Especially if you already own a small business those profits that you make in that business should be invested into bigger companies than yours.

But hey I'm not giving advice here. I'm just making street-smart sense. Now, let's continue to deposit those "racks." #Hussle

Now, between you, me, and the trees, I was earning plenty of cash at the time working as a stand-up comic. I didn't put that money into this account right away, but in the back of my mind I knew I was always earning amounts like this telling jokes. So, I had a buffer in case I did lose all the money. I knew I could earn the money back through my work and replace any losses or stay out the game altogether if I sucked at it, but I knew what I could risk. This is what I mean when I write that unless your situation was exactly like mine, your style and thinking will be different than mine was. It will depend on whatever your financial situation is at this present moment. The audience for this book is almost everybody, so we know we're all living differently, but what we can share and compare is what is similar about our stories of investing and trading.

So, armed with knowing I had an income, I started to learn everything under the sun on how to pick stocks.

And you will too, if you're getting anything out of reading this book. I read about "the trend," low PE's, undervalued stocks, buy low sell high, popular stocks, large caps, mid caps, small caps, micro caps, and nano caps and on and on. I got a journal to log all of my searches, write down my ideas, and track the money in the account. Although your broker's website will keep a record of your accounting online, that's nothing like doing it on paper yourself. Doing it yourself keeps you intimate with your money and reminds you to look at your risk/reward ratio on a daily basis. I suggest that all at-home hedge fund managers keep a journal. One day, your internet will crash on you and the only IT girl you know is on vacation. You'll be glad you put it all in a journal.

While you're at the store picking up a new journal for this journey, grab a couple more blank steno notebooks so you can do what is called "paper trading." I did this instinctively before I even heard they had a name for it, but paper trading is how we "stake out" a stock, hunt it down, and track it. Before entering a trade (buying it). This should become routine for you throughout your trading career. I just knew I should watch how the specific stock of choice moved and its price in the market during real time, following it as it zigged and zagged all day and seeing which stocks followed suit. Not much different than what some of us had to deal with on the "real streets." Staking out the next heist, hanging with hoes and drug dealers who are changing prices and relocating constantly and then the routine of the po-po. They had a routine and if you wanted to stay out of trouble (prison) it would be smart of you to know it. Because out there in the real world you can get caught up in some sh** you really didn't have nothing do with *this time*... if you're not up on game. So instead of roaming the streets these days I watch all of the action and price movement on the exchanges on my computer screens safe at my desk. Not trusting them the market makers but trusting yourself.

After doing all of this prep work to get ready to make my first trade, I realized I didn't know how to physically make a trade on my account using the brokerage's software, so I had to call it in and get tutored by them. I admit this to you because I don't want anything to hinder your will to save and make money now. Don't ever be embarrassed by anything you don't know in this game. With the internet, you can find most answers you might need.

Have you ever heard the tale about the time folks were trying to sue Thomas Edison or Einstein one of 'em for his invention money? The people around him said he was too crazy to handle all of his cash, and they wanted to take control of his money. There's always a clown to be found around money disguised as a relative or a lover. So, the prosecutor of the case asked Mr. Edison a question a kindergarten student could answer. He asked Edison, "Who discovered America?" Edison replied, "I don't know the answer to your question, but I have a library at home full of books, and I'm sure the answer is in one of them." The judge said, Sheeeeet, he ain't crazy, and granted him full control of his money. Well, the judge didn't say what I wrote, but he did give him full control of his money. I can't confirm the validity of this story. I heard it in high school and I googled it like I suggest to all of you when researching facts. The searches had nothing but mentioned Einstein. But it's a good one. I've always remembered it. As long as you get its meaning you know where I'm coming from. Do your own research and never be afraid especially when it comes to ***your money*** to search or ask your brokerage for information you don't know. #Please

I really can't talk about risk allocation without bringing up the over-the-counter (OTC) market, a.k.a. penny stocks. Realizing that some accounts will have to begin with a similar "principal" amount that I started with and share about in this literature you have in your hands; you will be easily drawn to this market. You'll think to yourself; I only have a little money to invest, and I want to maximize it as much as possible. So, you'll think if you pay pennies for a stock, maybe you can buy way more shares, get lucky, and flip it into thousands of dollars. Yeah, I'm laughing too. It's not going to work like that; the risk/reward is too high in that market. The companies we're looking for are actual productive and profitable businesses, and they aren't usually found on the OTC. Though there are some, such as Adidas and Tencent, but there are reasons these companies trade on this market. The ones I've mentioned are foreign companies and, though legit, they don't have to keep up with the standards and compliance of the other market indexes: Dow Jones, Nasdaq, NYSE,

AMEX, S&P, the Russell, and many more. Transparency isn't the OTC's thing. #Shade

You can actually find penny stocks on some of the more regulated exchanges as well, and the companies are held to a higher accountability with much more transparency. If you want to buy a penny stock, you should buy it off one of the bigger exchanges. I get why you might be tempted by penny stocks; I wouldn't discourage anyone from figuring out how to get money from them, but I will warn you that they are worth pennies for many reasons. Some are good reasons you can benefit from, like a reconstruction of the company or it getting bought out by a bigger company, but for the most part these stocks are "doo-doo." They might go bankrupt on you. Sometimes they may be under reconstruction, but then they go private and pay you less than pennies for the shares you held for so long hoping for something bigger. Doing your due diligence when buying into one of these companies is an absolute must. Doing due diligence on every stock is a must, but amp it up when it comes to these penny stocks. For me, I've only found value in them when they are a part of a hot sector like lithium, marijuana, gold, oil, and silver. Everything else in between is as "risky" as the 405 traffic in LA. Maybe you know somebody a relative or friend (known as an insider) who works at the company that's worth pennies, but he brags all the time about how they will be worth so much more in the future.

In such a case, you might want to take out a flier—which is a small position, not going all in—on them. I made some money in the beginning with a few penny stocks in the sectors that I already mentioned. I still own a few presently in these sectors, because success is duplicatable. I first consider my risk/reward. If I buy ten thousand shares of a stock for ten cents each, what could I make? I think, shoot, if it goes up even *eighty cents*, I will make ten thousand times eighty cents, or $8000.00 Spending $1,000 out of pocket to make $8,000...now that sounds like a pretty good risk/reward scenario. On the other hand, can you afford to buy 10,000 shares on one trade when you only have $1,000 to start with? You begin thinking that you can instead cut it in half or a quarter or whatever meets your risk threshold. What I like about trading is the math. If 10,000 shares of anything goes up twenty-five cents, we make $2,500 in that one trade. Dreams like this don't always come true, but the math is the math and participants keep trying. But let's snap back to reality. We shouldn't look forward to taking those kinds of trades until we have made plenty of money ourselves and we're able to risk whatever we want and reap big rewards every day.

For now, we stay small and dream big. If you learn properly on the way, you may stick to the disciplines you created when you had little money; that way, when the money becomes great, you've already perfected your "edge" and strategy for buying stocks. What I decided when I started to trade with my first $1,500 was that I could stomach losing $200 without a problem. I have dropped that kind of money on lesser-valued things, things I don't even use anymore, have thrown in the garbage or given away. Two hundred dollars wouldn't make my stomach turn if I lost it on something I truly believed in or thought I could profit from after doing my homework on the investment. I learned many years ago: I never really lose at anything if I learned how to do it better the next time. It's like trying a stunt on your skateboard, skis, or bike: you fail many times, but each time you learn how to do it better until you get it.

. . .

I began with this attitude that "failure wasn't an option," so I started off spending hours on researching, and still do, before putting on a trade. So, with $200 being the amount of money that I could lose, it's now my number that I could put on every trade and feel good about it. Once I had that number, I was free to start picking stocks with a pulse and profits. If I gave each trade $200, then I owned only five stocks at a time. A note about diversification: it's not only about diversifying the companies you invest into, it's also about the different indexes as well. Like I've written up top, you don't want to put all your money into one spot or one index either. #Diversify

I wanted to be sure my portfolio was diversified, so I was in WTI (oil), AG (silver), DRD (gold), and GPRO (drones and cameras). The penny stocks I got were in the marijuana sector, TRTC and CGRW at the time. I don't know where these stocks are today because I no longer own them or any of these positions that I'm sharing with you now. I've moved onward and upward. At the time, I also owned a couple of shares of SBUX (coffee) at its low and

FSLR (solar). I would sit back and watch these stocks return to the "mean" and profit me slowly. I was in and out of these stocks on the regular while I added contributions every week to my principal amount. After my portfolio began to swell, I started adding companies that pay me dividends and held them long enough (a year or longer) to incur what is famously known as "compound interest."

No matter what, I never break the rules I make. I never put more than $200 on one trade. If two shares of Apple (AAPL) cost more than $200, I would only buy one share and so on. Now, many of the other books on trading suggest that you use percentages when determining capital risk on any trade. I've heard anything from 2 percent to 5 percent of your entire account and every figure after that. If you're a math whiz, you could go about it using percentages. I'm a "gut" person, and I know how much of a kick I can take in my gut (it's a matter of perspective for each of us). I've been kicked in the gut so many times in my life, it's a good thing I have strong abs. #SixPack

. . .

So, for me it was and always will be about the amount of money I can stomach to lose on any trade or investment. When I get to seven figures, then I can see the percentage formula being useful. But this is how I began building my account, and I hope my story makes your story easy to write. Once my account had over $3,000 in it, I would follow my same rules, always keeping a third out in cash and allocating the rest according to my risk threshold on that day or week. I'm never all in, and I would always suggest that you never be all in either. In less than seven months, I had used these techniques to grow my account to over five figures, $13,000 to be exact.

The uncertainty in the market is a "bear," and it could snatch your money up on any given day. You wake up to a bright and sunny morning, and your account is worth half of what it was before you went to bed. But because you stayed patient and stuck to your rules, you kept cash on hand while the rest of your money was working for you. Since the market has crashed, you can now buy the stocks you've already invested into that you know and believe are sound companies at lower prices; that's called "reducing cost basis." Or pick up some deal on a company you've always wanted to invest in at its lowest price in years. Then, when the market wakes up from its crash and corrects itself (as always), you can cash in and win, win, win. #Profits

Note: if you're looking to earn huge returns or get rich in the market, you want to be around when the market crashes. I keep cash on hand for this very reason. J. Livermore also said that every bull market must end, and it will end badly. You get it, right? You want the market to "crash" while you're in the market; knowing what you know, you could get paid huge for sticking it out. Every crash in stock market history has risen again to even newer heights.

If you're one of the lucky ones to be there when it does, and you have a cool hand, you can make yourself a rich person. Rich folks want the market to crash so they can take advantage of this type of event; it makes them richer and you poorer, because you didn't know this information for a fact. You might have assumed it, but knowing it prepares you to take advantage of it when it actually happens. Many times, buying a stock isn't what's important when it comes to making huge profits in the market. It's *what you paid* for that stock that is important. #TheEdge

When you learn how to do this, you'll be turning losers into winners for the rest of your wealthy life.

THE TRADE ENTRY

FIRST THING ABOUT ENTERING A TRADE: nine times out of ten, it's going to go against you, so know that. Drill it into your strategy. So many of these social media traders are trading quickly and with debt; that's why they talk about losing so much and taking losses and implementing "stop-losses." It's because they're losing money.

They also borrow money to trade yeah if your credit is good, they'll let you trade on margin. I would highly advise against that, especially when you have little money that's growing up to be big. Using leverage and margin to make money are for those with a huge cash reserve to cover their losses. Many traders and even some brokerage firms play the game when they know they don't have that kind of reserve, so they just gamble and end up losing their accounts and firms in many cases. Tha's why you hear those stories of greedy folks offing themselves and leaving their families broke or going to prison. That's not my thing in this game and it shouldn't be yours either. It's also not my business usually. Whatever happens to these folks will have no effect on my positions or objectives in these markets. It's just news and noise. I don't like to lose money unless it's profitable. If I'm losing money, it has to be for a profit somewhere else. #Rotation

I'm not saying I haven't lost money. Surely, I have, and lots of it, but not in the stock market. What I'm saying is that losing money is not normal, and you shouldn't think it is. You will hear and read all the time talk from other traders about losing money like it is normal, like you should get used to it. (No wonder they call the non-pros "suckers" and "dumb money;" if you believe that shit, you dumb. #ThatPart)

· · ·

I believe that's a terrible mindset and strategy for any trader to start out with. Who's in this to lose? Like there's some fu**ing award show passing out awards to losers. #DontThinkSo

I'll repeat it ova and ova: a stock is going to go against you, but that doesn't mean it's a loser. It's down, not out, it's like what I tell my gurl. I'm down baby but I'm not out. I can do other things for ya. Assuming you did all of your work (due diligence) applying your edge with patience. Over time, that stock will go back in the direction of making profits for you. It will turn its butt right around and climb higher, with or without you. Your stock is not a loser until you sell your position at a loss, as in less than what it cost you to buy the position. #Duh

Keep your stop-loss in your fu**ing heads (mental stop-losses). Do not set your stop-loss in your brokerage account. Warning. That's lazy. And you will surely get stopped out. #Algos

· · ·

Remember, it's only you. You're not in those real streets right now, and you're not working for anyone else but you. So, the only one that's going to fu** you up is you. You might say to yourself, *I should kick my own ass*, but you don't.

Preparing yourself to lose is counterproductive to me. Many of the Wall Street traders and even many traders who work from wherever they're posted up will unapologetically berate you and other people they don't know on social media and in their blogs for not taking losses. Not you personally but it will feel personal when they do it. Because it's usually unsolicited advice and it's not for every investor. Surely some of these traders need to get out of their trades because they loss by thinking they knew how to trade. Day traders don't usually consider or care what the companies are doing they only focus on the trade the spread for that day. Those of us with smaller accounts cannot afford to day trade not really you can get lucky but sooner or later probably sooner when you experience your first loss, you'll chose a more reliable strategy. And that's if you're not the kind of person that gives up on themselves a lot. A quitter.

. . .

Your objectives should put you back in line. We must learn to invest and let our money grow as quickly or slowly as the market deems. Just never buy something you're not going to outlive. See, the insane part about it is these smarter than you folks go on posting on these social media sites about cutting loses without explaining what they consider a losing stock is. What's your personal reason for adding a stop-loss? Because it may have nothing to do with me and how I'm trading or investing into these markets. Furthermore, these pajama traders and self-proclaimed big shots are painting with broad strokes and that paint can get on the vulnerable new person and blow their account out.

We're supposed to just take their word for it because they've studied this sh** in labs and forums that they never invite main street to. So, they sound so "smart." We couldn't afford their summits even if we were invited. Davos (it's in Sweden, homie) cost like 250K to show up and 100K annually to get an invite. And do you think they're considering all of us while there having these forums that none of us can afford to go to? If it isn't in their portfolio, why should they care if you or I cut losses? What are they like the NBA now "WE CARE?" No, they don't. They don't give a rats ass 'bout us or our losses or wins. Game recognize game here.

They say they're helping you. And I say why? Why do they give a fu**? I believe it's to fu** you up and cause you to sell and lose money to them. I have the experience to speak on it. Now you can either lose or learn to "wait for it." Like W.B. says all the time (Warren Buffett). It's like a batter up to swing. You don't and shouldn't swing at every pitch; you wait for the right one to cross the plate, and then you give it all you got. I know you can strike out if we want to talk baseball but that's entirely different than just handing over your money. You're going to have to bankrupt your billion-dollar corporation to get my money. I know they won't do it intentionally. Well, maybe they won't, but I'm not to take it personally if they do. Imagine thinking a 2-billion-dollar company on purpose bankrupting itself just to take mines and yours thousand-dollar investment our five shares of whatever. I DON'T THINK SO. And when you think about it, you'll know it too. Bankruptcy does happen companies go bankrupt, but you would know that because you've been doing the due diligence to know that. Again, you do you here. If you buy into losing, well that's an oxymoron, then you have the stomach to live with it. #MOS

Your stock will head in the other direction at some period of time while you're in the trade but guess what: it will also turn back and go in the direction of making you profits. Wait for it! If it zigs, it zags. Lock that into your strategy notes, will ya? (And remember to look up the mean reversion while you're at it.) These down times are also an opportunity to buy your excellent stock picks at a better price using what is called "reducing cost basis." If your buy was great at \$18, let's say it's an even better value at \$9, a 50 percent discount. Maybe... as long as the story hasn't changed about the stock you own (a crash indi-cator is the 50 percent drop). We could deep dive this topic, but I think the only time the term "deep dive" should be used is in a porno. Every time I hear the analysts using that phrase "deep dive," I see porn stars. I'm joking here of course, because I shared with you at the beginning of this book that any topic that needed further explanation, you should look it up...

but you don't have to get that deep. I didn't want to waste your reading time with a lot of fancy phrases and mathematics like so many other books have done because really you can read those too, somebody has already written most of those books and you should read them as if your money depended on it because it probably will. If you want to become excellent at investing your money, I highly recommend you read all the books you can enjoy about this industry. Self-taught is better than never learning at all and it's more profitable. I've certainly have read over a hundred books easy.

The *Wall Street-Smarts* series are books to *shift* you into the right gear and to encourage you to get in the game. I prefer to make you laugh and not stress you out about the market movements using words like *plunge, surge, fallout*. Everything isn't so serious in the stock market like the hype men and women on TV make it sound. No one's in a hurry. No one is scurrying around the stock exchange floor anymore except them (pre-Rona covid19) because they only have an hour to do the show. The stock exchanges are serious about their traditions so there's a bell at the opening of markets but don't let the bell get you emotionally caught up. It's there to represent the beginning and the end of the traditional trading day. There is pre-market trading and after-hour trading. You can do this if you wish through your broker, but the traditional trading day is done between the bells. Nevertheless, the bell is their idea. It has no effect on the stocks you buy, and it should have no effect on you at home. If you clap with the folks at the closing bell, hopefully you're clapping because you followed your rules, stuck to the strategy you've decided on, and traded well. You're clapping because they didn't take your money today. #GoodReason

Research is Your New Best Friend

Searching the internet is a new human habit; now you can use any search engine to find out about most anything. You know we all like Google, but don't be afraid to mix it up some with Yahoo, Bing, and others. Sometimes you could find related or conflicting data. Most traders search through data just to confirm what they themselves think, but you, my thousandaire, should search through data to discover what others are thinking. What *you* think really shouldn't matter to you more than what the other participants in the market are thinking. #Edge

Other uses for data would be researching the businesses you're interested in buying into and growing with. Spend time learning their stock history and its movements, but mostly understand the fundamentals of the business so you can make an informed decision before investing into them.

In this book, I wanted to get right to the heart of people like me who are usually discouraged from investing in the stock market because of the bullshit. I want to encourage you, not discourage you. We can overcome the bullshit. #Friend

So, back to the topic of trade entry. Once you have learned about the "mean," understood that whatever zigs will also zag, and found a strategy of trading that works for you, you will see for yourself how often the so-called losers become winners. Most of the time (highest probability), this is because it wasn't a loser in the first fu**ing place. It was you listening to these fancy jerks spewing all their technical talk because they want to make their money by getting you to sell your positions at a loss. See, if a seller can get you to sell at a loss, it's then a buy for that seller. The way new traders (retail traders, that's us) are manipulated to lose money by the media, blogs, and Twitter just makes me want to write these books even more since there's no way to kick the asses of everybody on Wall St. who calls us at-home hedge fund managers suckers and "dumb money." These folks do everything you can imagine to take your money through every media outlet possible. It just sends me batty, but it also made me pivot and write this book. Remember, the rest of the participants in this game—institutions, hedge funds, market makers—are on the other side of your trades, and they are in this to take your money.

Let's not let them. On the real streets, you wouldn't let anybody, especially someone without a weapon, just come up and take your money, would you? Why let these fools do it? Let us be the ones who learn to take theirs. Thousandaires for life! Like the dodgeball game, the playoffs, or any other activity, everyone and everything isn't gonna make it. Every stock isn't gonna make it either. Every corporation won't be profitable; many will bankrupt. Don't buy businesses you know nothing about. #StayInYourLane

Unlike in other games where there is a clear winner and a clear loser, in the stock market, it's not so clear. There are averages, percentages, more like the games in Vegas. One good hand, one lucky pull of the slot machine, can make up for any losses you may have incurred while playing the other games. So could one profitable stock buy. Why encourage taking losses when some of your ideas will probably be bad ones and you'll lose money anyways? The problem with Vegas is that it's a gamble; the risk/reward is usually too high, and you have no way of measuring it. In the stock market, you do have a way to measure risk/reward. In the stock market, you don't have to gamble because others are. You can learn to be a good investor and in control of your risk. You only have to have more profitable stocks than unprofitable ones. Sh** if you buy ten stock positions and six are profitable and the other four aren't you will still make money. Others would word this exact scenario as winning positions versus losing positions and screaming at you to sell the losing ones. But where I'm from I don't see it that way. You're either making me money or you're not and maybe not yet depending on your skills, services and value. And of course, time in the market. How much time do you give your investment to make you money? Just because you're not making money right now if I get an itch, I might cut you for something better but I will not lose money on ya. I might have to take less to get more but take a loss is just a weird way to suggest to do business. If I believe in what I'm doing and what I'm spending my money on I will wear it out before I take a loss. You will have to disappear with my money. And believe me some of these companies I have invested into over the years have done just that but that's what I expect from them. So no surprise and no willingly losing money. Otherwise I wouldn't have sunk my money into the business in the first place. We've all been taken before no reason to make a big deal out of it or promote it and scare young and old retail traders out of their money. And why not? Why shouldn't they be allowed to play you? It's a game. Remember that and you'll stay paid. #RiskManagement

. . .

You take a hit you move on and make even more money with a better company. Not as easy as it sounds? That's what they're paid to say about every-thing they make hard before it's easy. We as humans love to complicate the simplest of actions. Buy low, sell high. How they've complicated the hell out of that. How I grew up it would be a bad idea to think of yourself as a loser maybe it's because every day growing up on main street, we've witnessed so many losses in real life. And getting shot isn't fun at all. Somehow, we had to win to get out. Oh yeah. I've been shot before.

This is a zero-sum game off the top. Don't let anyone tell you, you can't play it and be profitable. What's profitable for you isn't profitable for everyone we don't all start out on the same starting line. Get ready, set, go from where you stand. I'm sure no one would think I had more money than they had, and they'd probably be right. My money is my money it cannot equate to your money.

I think the system would be very afraid if the other half of Americans started to understand where the money is and took the time to take what they could earn out of it. It's been like one of those movies where they hide the treasure right in front of our faces for most of our lives but because it's been made invisible to us with illusions of greed and fear, so we can't see it or benefit from it. Especially when they get regular folks in a protest frenzy. If you remember "Occupy Wall Street" there's no way through anger that we would see anything for what it was or how it could benefit even those protesters.

That in a sense if we really wanted to protest, we do it by taking their money that they put out in front of us every day of the week "rob the rich" legally. It's not a robbery with violence like in that show on Netflix *Money Heist* obviously too much risk. Instead it's with a collective of wits, "street-smarts" and patience. You do realize these folks keep putting this money in the air for public consumption. Maybe we should consume it? I'm a living example of this. At the time of this writing, protests are currently happening in the streets and I have chosen not to be in those streets. Instead I'm using my protest to hip people to the game to improve their financial situations. #BLM

. . .

Gamblers gamble in the stock market too because it's what they do. It's who they are. Let them gamble but not you, not the thousandaire, not someone who wants to take control of their finances. That takes discipline, not gambling. My hope for you is that you decide not to gamble but to invest and manage your finances according to your own personal objectives. And you can believe there will be others lurking on Wall St. to lead you right down that path of gambling in options, futures, penny stocks, and other tools. They will offer you some new strategy or trading system you can buy *just from them*. Forget that! You've worked too hard to become a thousandaire. You finally made it, and now you have plenty of spending money. Then someone calls or emails you, inviting you to look at this "hot new system" that they created to make you a better trader. Really? I've seen it, I've heard it, and I don't want that to be you. It's a quick way to turn your winners into losers.

At the beginning, you'll think someone is trying to screw you out of your money. Especially if you come from where most of us come from: Main Street, a.k.a.

the real streets. We hate to get burnt! We're not psychologically prepared for the market at the beginning. Another reason for getting this book into your hands is to prepare you mentally and physically for anything. This series can help you become adaptable to getting this money and not getting scared out of it. A scared person cannot win.

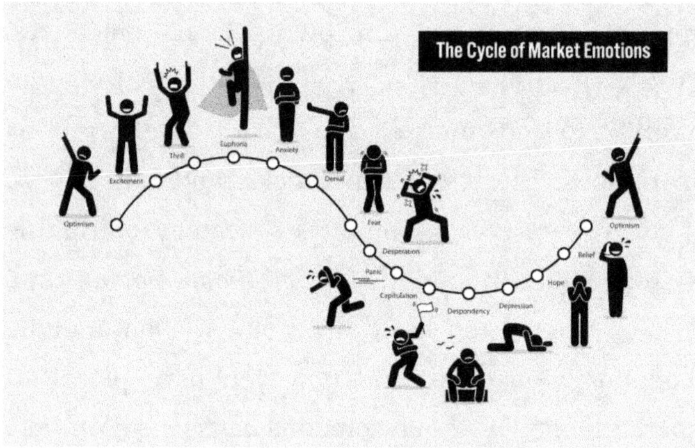

Let me attempt to form a new perception of investing for you if I haven't already. Sometimes all it takes to turn losers into winners is to change your perception of stocks (corporations) to determine what your risk/reward will be. A complete change in perception can give you confidence in each and every trade or investment you add to your fund.

Again, we're going to ask ourselves some questions (never stop asking questions). The first is this: do you have $177? It's funny, when a family member or a friend asks me if they should get into the stock market, I start by asking this question. The looks on their faces are Instagram-worthy, with some of 'em thinking I'm asking them for money. #Lol

I say, "No, I don't need the money. I want to know if you have $177?" Almost everyone I ask says yes, and I kind of believe they mean maybe, but I go with the yes. Let's say you the reader are saying yes also. Well, at the time I'm writing this book, AAPL (Apple) stock closed today at $177 a share. I ask you again, do you have $177 extra cash? If the answer is yes, who do you think will earn more money with "your" $177 this year? You? Or Apple!? I love this question because it breaks you down simplistically. Go ahead, answer the question.

. . .

It's Apple, right? Well, then, why don't you call up one of these brokers and let them know you'll be buying your first share of Apple? You've just made your first intelligent investment. That was easy, right? No! For some reason, people don't get it, end up spending that $177 on something that won't make them money, and then have nothing to show for it. Whatever product they bought, whomever they helped out, or whichever club they went to, that cash—a.k.a. investment—is gone forever. Now you have to go back to work to get more money when you could've had that lil' amount of money making you more money now.

And just to add fuel to the fire by the time I was able to drop these series of books onto the Amazon platform. Apple's stock has hit over 300.00 for the second time since that price. I sold it at 323.00 before it went back to 276.00 and now back over 300.00. I suspect by the time these books drop the stock will be lower again and ready for reentry before going any higher in the years to come. It's as simple as understanding and knowing these movements of different stocks by being in the market.

Being out of the market you know nothing. #WallStGame

Has your perception shifted a little; can you see what I have described? You probably already possess some intuitive know-how if you're asking the right questions. This question was easier than most, but we all know Apple will make more money than all of us reading this book at the same time. #Honest

Now, in this example, we found some extra capital to get in the game, though not much if we were only talking $177. But, again, I'm making a point. And oh, in case you missed it, yes, you can buy one share of stock at a time. This should help you get a better perception of why you and I should be invested. You don't have to be a billionaire or want to be one either to make profits in the market. To know this game is to keep money, with "you" always in a constant flux. This Wall Street Game isn't only for the richest in the land; it's especially made for you and for us all. Because if you were smart enough to answer yes to a simple question like the one above, you must have some past, future, and recent knowledge of the corporation I was speaking of (Apple). You're probably a customer (my family is). These are questions you must ask yourself anytime you invest in anything. The answers will come to you, and if they don't and you're unable to find out the answers you want, "Don't do it, dog." Don't trade that day.

Never be afraid to ask in business, *Will this money make more money with me or with them* (the investment)? I don't care if you're looking at real estate or Uncle Joe's "weed shop," what will be the return on your capital (ROC) if you give them your money? Nothing else matters but whether this investment will make you M-O-N-E-Y!

If the money stays with you, it has some protection, but it can't do much. Most likely, it will get spent on useless stuff and not put to work making you more money. Because the truth is that most of us have no plans in growing or building a corporation, and I'd rather buy a piece of an already successful corporation and let it work for me anyway. #WayOf-TheTurtle

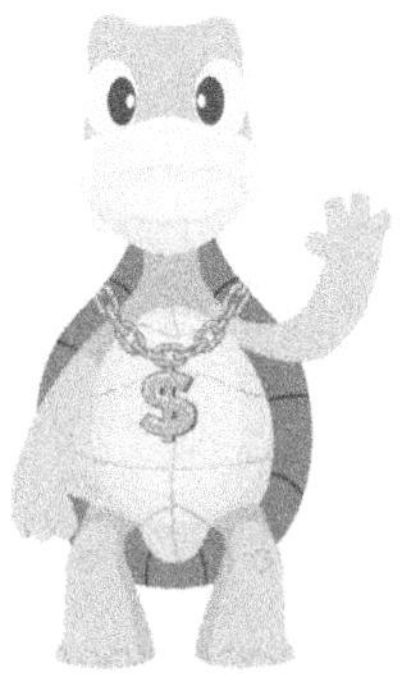

Your money will be saved and stagnate, but it's not working for you until you put it to work. Investing even when you don't have much money is better than padding a savings account because, for one, it's hard to save when you have nothing in mind to buy or just because people tell you that you should have a savings account. It's probably linked to why the average American can't keep even $400 extra in any of those accounts.

Furthermore, when someone saves for the purpose of a "rainy day," you can be sure a storm is comin' for the exact amount of money they have saved for that rainy day, give or take a dollar or two. Can I get a witness?! How many of you have held onto cash just to have to give it away to a family member, church, or a weekend at Coachella? Or, the best yet, your brother or sister needs bail or a gall bladder operation, and their request for your money is $8 less than all the money you have been saving in that account for the last year. You've saved $1,000, and they need only $992 of it to get out. #KeepingItReal

I say enjoy spending profits instead of pennies. Put the money you work so hard for to work for a lifetime. Just be sure that, before entering a trade, you check your emotions with the hostess. If you're lucky and disciplined emotionally, financially, and personally, you can learn to turn losers into winners and then help someone else do the same in the future. Maybe your son, daughter, or grandkids. #PayIt-Forward

How to Make Your First Trade

In the "Risk Allocation and Money Management" chapter, I laid out how I managed to trade my first thousand dollars. Here, I'd like to add more to the story of how I got my account in the first place and started to trade with just $1,500.

Trading a small amount of money is fun, if it's all the money you're starting out with and you're twelve years old. But it isn't that much fun when you're eighty! Simply put, it's hard to trade with "little money." I think age would be the gauge for the degree of pain you would be feeling. A twelve-year-old with $1,000 to invest is feeling pretty good about himself. He has his whole life in front of him, but his challenge is that he's got no experience at life. When you come in to start with a thousand bucks in, let's say, your thirties, forties, or fifties, it might seem discouraging, even a lil' embarrassing, but you have an edge that a twelve-year-old doesn't, and that's **experience**. With it, you can speed things up and meet your objectives. You were a cat before they were kittens. Living experience is your first edge.

Briefly, I will tell you that I learned how to get into the market and start trading from a trader friend of mine who used to manage millions of dollars for the firm where he was working. He asked me one day, "Do you know you can trade on your own dime?" I'm like, "Whaaat?" Because back then, I didn't know I could do anything but give people like Morgan & Stanley my money to manage my everyday spending. Not one of 'em ever suggested I should or could trade my own account.

I shit you not.

When I met my trader friend, he was doing his own thing in Century City, CA. He had recognized me from television, and we quickly became friends because we both like to talk about money. We had that in common, except he felt I could learn to do better financially. I don't know why he thought that, but I was grateful he did. He actually walked me into a Fidelity brokerage office in Century City and made sure I opened the proper accounts: a Roth IRA and an individual transfer on death (TOD) cash management account. This way, I could trade and remain absolutely liquid. I felt it necessary then—and still do—to have my cash available to me at all times. With the TOD account, you even get an ATM card and you can tiptoe into a bank and pull out a few grand if you need it. Then tiptoe out.

Back then, I was already used to what I thought was first-class treatment at banks and other places that would recognize me from television or some film I had done. I had personal assistants helping me open bank accounts along the way in my career, but I never really took to banks like most folks. I used them because we had to, right? And the metal box under the bed was no longer sufficient, so I had to use a bank. But when you start making too much money (if that's even a thing...I think it is), then you find out that there are all these different kinds of banks. This one bank used to drop checks off at my house for me before I left on tour or for whatever I was spending it on. Just like many of you, I had never seen no sh** like that before I had become a "professional spender." Most Americans have been conditioned to spend, spend, spend but never to invest. Just keep spending to make other investors wealthy. Now, I'm not blaming the institutions (okay, maybe a lil', but not much), but back then I was like, *I need to learn how to flip my money legally; there must be a better way.* So, believe me when I tell you that I appreciate this brother for informing me, I could do it myself.

See, the thing is that he made me feel good and secure about opening an account with only $1,500. To be honest with you guys, I didn't trust financial institutions very much (I am from the real streets, really), so I opened my first account with this small amount to audition them "quiet as kept" and to see if I could trust these folks to transact business with a guy like me.

Furthermore, there was no going online and easily setting up these accounts like you can do today. I'm glad they fixed that for the novice investor. It's so easy to think you don't belong in this big ocean of sharks and whales, and maybe you don't; it's not up to me to make that decision for you. I'm just here as evidence, as proof, that you may be wrong about that. They need us and we need them to keep the money continuously circulating in a constant flux like it has for many moons. #Contributions

. . .

FYI, Fidelity actually prefers you to open your smaller accounts online these days if your deposit/contribution is less than $50K. They will explain to you the differences between the accounts. (I'm sure TD Ameritrade, Charles Schwab and others are helpful too, I'm just not familiar with any of them like I am with "Fi'" and Morgan & Stanley. Neither one of these institutions pay me to recommend them; I'm just cool like that because I want *you all to have a go-to immediately* and know you will get help setting up your accounts.) They call your deposits "contributions." I'm thinking it's because you're "contributing" to yourself by continually adding money to your account. See, poor people (with poor thinking) deposit money. Rich folk (with rich thinking) contribute to their accounts. It's like the gas gauge in an expensive car; it's never on "empty," it's in "reserve." #Mindset

You're allowed to set up any schedule you'd like for your contributions. If you want to contribute to yourself once a week, twice a month, every two months, you can. How cool is that you get to contribute to yourself as often as you'd like. I hope you like yourselves. Surely, you'll want to contribute to you, because you are the one who deserves to keep your money. The more money you want to have, the more you will contribute and invest into you. You're the business now. #PayYouFirst

This is unlike your regular banks, where you probably already make regular deposits, because a bank doesn't pay you for being with them; you're actually being charged fees for the pleasure of their services (I say that loosely because they're really a parking space for petty cash, as far as I'm concerned) to manage your debt and your spending. #Bankstas

WAY OF THE TURTLE AND TRADING PLACES

I'M GOING to guess our readers would be more familiar with the movie *Trading Places* than they would the book, *Way of the Turtle*. I say this because that was me. Though *Way of the Turtle* has been available in print for many years, most folks on Main Street have never heard of it. Most of us have seen *Trading Places*, however. Well, supposedly the inspiration for this film came from this book. It's a philosophy known amongst most of the elite folks and accepted as an intelligent philosophical belief, but down here on Main Street, we're not taught these philosophies, how to implement them in our lives, or why we should. It's not something you hear about in the hood. #WallStGame

· · ·

An abbreviated explanation of this philosophical practice is that it's a gathering of many bright people who clearly won't "all" make it to the top of the heap but getting close to the top can be just as satisfying and profitable. Another way I interpret it is that to become a great leader, you'll have to become a great follower and know who the heck you're following. #Mentors

Nevertheless, on Main Street, it's the opposite, with stimulates like television, magazines, billboards, and radio. We're all conditioned to chase what we most likely will never be or have ourselves. We're taught that we ALL can become millionaires and billionaires like them, every one of us. #NotTrue

I'll give you another story of why who you follow matters, taken from personal experience. I have many facets to my story as an actor/stand-up comic and writer/producer. I wasn't unlike many inspiring stand-up comics. I wanted to be like Richard Pryor mostly, then I got to know him personally opening up with him at the *World Famous Comedy Store* in the original room and main room. Hanging out drinking and smoking I really got to love this dude. Knowing him was a surreal experience for me. I grew up listening to all his sh** and now I'm standing next to him... talking to him, like we were on the same level, when I knew we were not. It was bananas. Though I sprinkled myself with some George Carlin and Robin Williams too both of these dudes weren't only great comics, but they were great people too. They were always kind to me. I love them all, but I really related to Richard. We had a lot in common. By coincidence, I could look a lot like him too. I even had a taped audition to play him before producers started getting into trouble in this town, but I did the taping anyway (I still have that script and tape). I thought of it as an honor just to be asked to do it.

What I want to say to you is that I emulated a great comic and human being that didn't always do great things. I did the drugs and alcohol, had the women, got paid a good deal of money, and had plenty of stage time all over the country to live like he did. And I did. To keep this brief, obviously you want to avoid following the wrong person no matter how great they may seem to be in the public eye or in your own eyes. Their reality is what you should be looking at—how they live, how they treat others, and, most of all, how they treat themselves. Then make a decision if you want your life or theirs.

Michael J. Fox said in an interview that if we all sat in a circle, threw each of our major problems in the middle of the circle, and could choose any of the other problems, he believes we would all take ours back and live with them. I agree. Do you?

Cool, now, let me share with you my understanding of *Way of the Turtle*, and then I encourage you to go and buy the book ASAP. I mean it like how the police mean it when they ask you to get out of the car. It's up to you what happens next.

Now, the story of the *Way of the Turtle*

is much like the premise of the film *Trading Places*, so go ahead and search for the film, then sit back and get ready to learn, earn, and laugh.

An inside note: seeing that movie years ago is one of the reasons I chose acting instead of trading back then. I thought I would've been a better casting choice than Eddie, so I headed to Hollywood. I had a job interview in San Francisco for a stockbroker gig before going to Hollywood, but that's a story for another book. I bring it up because I thought it would be easier to act like a broker than to actually become one. I was correct. I'm still not a broker, but I would play one on TV. Now, I do manage thousands of dollars on the stock exchange every day, and I still continue to act as well. Weird how it all kind of manifested itself in reverse. I wished I had known this business of trading and managing money like I do today before making a dime in show business. #NoRegrets

Anyway, this is how the turtle story goes (I'm taking some liberty with my memory, but here's the nutshell version): this rich white dude (obviously, nobody black was rich in the markets back then) named Richard Dennis went to a turtle farm in Singapore. What he actually witnessed while at the turtle farm was a pond full of turtles, and what caught his eye and curiosity was that there were huge tortoises amongst the little ones. As he saw the turtles of all sizes interacting with each other, he noticed that not only were they meticulously slow, taking their time going to wherever it was that they were going, but they would speed up when necessary or attacked.

Now, the tiny turtles got to ride on the backs of the bigger turtles, which Richard found simplistically brilliant because those little turtles riding on bigger turtles' backs ate what they ate. See, those big ol' turtles could reach up to the higher shrubbery and eat them easily. The little guys riding on their backs were now at that height and able to eat the food the bigger turtles ate. Without the huge tortoises allowing these little guys to ride on their backs, they could never reach the shrubbery to eat as well as the big guys do. They would have to wait for the leaves to fall to the ground (and be bottom feeders) in order to eat as well.

Also, the tiny turtles got to travel on the big guys and enjoy the same places together. Wherever the big guys traveled, the little ones had the same view of higher ground. So, when they traveled together, they all had window seats in first class. From observation, we know those little turtles will never be the size of the big ones, but it didn't mean they had to aspire to be as big as they could never be. As long as they could get on the back of or follow a bigger turtle, they could enjoy the very life he/she was enjoying. Now, this philosophy is taught to elites but not on Main Street and certainly not in the hood. This book you're reading might be the only book to ever catch the eye of a reader from the hood or Main Street. It's why I'm slipping you this info, so you can be up on the Wall St. game. So you can learn what they know before plowing your money into the stock market.

. . .

Before we move on, let me make clear that the *Way of the Turtle* philosophy is separate from the challenge of teaching anyone how to trade profitably, which was the real premise of the program and the film *Trading Places*. Now, I'm not saying the *Way of the Turtle* is the end all, be all, I'm just saying these kinds of missing pieces in our education and philosophical views can make moving forward from where I'm from difficult. Many don't take it this far in the hood; they're not aware that they can, but maybe now they can. And there's no wonder why over 50 percent of the American population doesn't have $400 to its name. Or that less than 50 percent of Americans even attempt to be in the markets. They're discouraged by all the highfalutin talk, and my hope for this book is to encourage as many of you as I can to ignore it all and get this money. The *Way of the Turtle* philosophy could be taught to all students in America through a children's book, but it hasn't been done so yet. Maybe I'll write that one too. Call it *Wall Street Smarts for Kids*— a cleaner version.

Bottom line: *everybody* doesn't need to push themselves so hard for an unrealistic lifestyle. #Kardashians

Now, the turtle program—or more like the turtle bet—was where the idea of the movie came from, with the philosophy and concept of the turtles intact in Mr. Dennis' mind. Richard Dennis had a buddy named William, and they made a bet amongst each other. Dennis, more so than William, believed he could teach anyone to trade profitably. It's funny when you hear the interviews and read the books about the turtles and they talk about how diverse their group was. This was then and not now.

The diversity they speak of didn't include race—no Blacks, Latinos or the stereotypical smart Asians. Their diversity back then had to do with intelligence and skills mostly, and then of course the diversity of the markets and portfolio management. They only saw green, if any color at all, and of course "the trend" of the markets. #Money

So when you're watching the movie *Trading Places*, remember that in Hollywood, when writing a movie, the question writers ask themselves sometimes is, *What if? What if a Black guy plays the role? What if we let an Asian fella do it?* And that's how Eddie Murphy got the role. My favorite scene that hits me every time with a Black American wake-up call takes place in the bathroom, where the ol' rich guys are discussing returning Dan Aykroyd's

 and Eddie Murphy's characters back to where they found them before the wager. And Don Ameche's character says to Ralph Bellamy as articulate as a line can be delivered, "Do you think I would let a nigger run this business?" Answer: nooooooo. Nothing changes until it actually changes, so I made some changes in this new age and got my own.

The crazy part is that most Americans haven't realized yet that they can—and should—easily get their own sh** too. It's not about becoming anything

you're not; it's about claiming your personal financial freedom. And not allowing anyone to make you think you can't have a piece of it in this era, because that's a damn lie. Shoot, you can start tonight if you have your own computer, and I know most of you do because I keep seeing folks using them to take pictures instead of making money. In my day, if we had computers in our pockets, we'd be living in an even more advanced world. It was my generation that helped create this one where you can have conversations with other people on your wristwatch. Side note: I really like my watch.

It would give me extra happiness if I found out that the youth and those from the real streets a.k.a. Main Street and the 50 percent of Americans (including millennials) who don't have the extra $400 in their account got this book. When I say, "got this book," I don't mean that you bought this book, even though I hope you did, but you could be borrowing it from your boss. I mean that you "get" the process that's being shared with you from my experience in the markets as an at-home hedge fund manager.

. . .

Before we wrap up this chapter, don't forget to purchase the book *Way of the Turtle*; it will serve you well. The mathematical formulas in the book were difficult for me for the most part; I don't quite understand all the math. I hope you're better at math than I am, and if so, then you will probably be more profitable than I am too (see, you have an edge already), which is a good thing. Of course, I won't know anything about it. I'm set in my own objectives. Just know, you don't have to be a math whiz in today's market to be profitable and a thousandaire.

THE MATH

STRAIGHT UP, I'm not well versed in all the different math equations that are used in the markets (to discourage non-pros I believe, jokingly), and forget about the taxes; I leave those to an accountant. What I know is my bottom line and how much money I have on hand (liquid) on any given day. #Happy

There are a bunch of mathematicians on the other side of your trades. Scientists, too. I would kid you not that some of the smartest minds in the world are on the other side of that trade you're about to take, and it's kind of cool knowing you can develop your own edge that profits you while you're investing among these great minds. Then you also have the algorithms. I have no idea what these machines are up to; well, I do, but it doesn't matter until they cause a "flash crash" or something, which never lasts longer than a flash. But it does scare the heck out of the gamblers in the market because of the margin calls and leverage. #PayUpToday

I can tell you that what I do know is how to *take* a profit. Pay whatever the tax structure is that year and come out with more money than I came in with. Period. #Uncomplicated

I know if I buy something for $42 and sell it for $52, I just made $10. This is the kind of basic math you'll need to know. Elementary, my friends. When it comes to buying or selling stock, get familiar with the terms in the market, like what an "ask" price is and what a "bid" price is. There will be talk of "slippage," and then there's the fee for making a trade. Oh yeah, you're charged a fee to buy or sell a stock; that's how the brokerage firms make some of their money. Say, for example, your brokerage charges a commission of $5 to buy your stock and then the same commission to sell it; that's a total of $10 to buy and sell one share or as many shares of stock that you want to buy or sell. So when taking those profits I speak of, you'll have to clear the commission price of $10. Let's go again. We buy a stock for $42 and sell it for $52. Just for laughs, if this example were true and it were actually one single share of stock, you would break even after paying the commission. You'd make nothing. But let's say you paid for ten shares times $42, which equals $420, and you sell them at $52 each times ten, which equals $520. After paying the commission of $10, you make $90. It's really that simple if you *keep* it simple.

By the time this book comes out, I predict commissions for buy and sell will be dropped to zero for most brokerage houses because in today's market the competitors are outdoing one another for your business. #Robinhood

---

Though there are mathematicians and scientists in this market who will blow your mind with their math, I believe it's a blind attempt to keep the novices out. *I must add here a warning to you the readers: don't let paying others for what they provide in the market discourage you.* So, don't be afraid to pay someone for their services if it will help you make money. "Give some, get some." I know a lot of homies who don't like to pay others for their services, so instead, they stay broke. #Selfish

---

Everyone deserves to make money. You make money off of them, and they make money off of you. That's okay; that's how the game is played, and everyone stays paid. #Circulation

---

Anyway, they have this math you'll hear often in accounting called the GAAP, an acronym that means "generally accepted accounting principles."

How crazy is that? Generally accepted accounting principles! Who's accepting this crap? How about some specific accounting principles (a new acronym: SAP)?

See what I mean? They throw you off with their math and wording (general semantics) so you feel like you don't know what they're talking about. And for the most part, we don't know, but we can pick it up quickly. Why would you ever think you can beat these guys? If you like the sorta thing as crazy math computations, then get into it, but if you're about saving money and having money grow in a fund in a consistent way, then keep it simple. Buy something for less and sell it for more. #Boom

It really is that easy. Don't let some "greater fool" convince you otherwise. What's not easy and is underestimated by many new traders and investors is that you and your emotions are your greatest asset or enemy. Controlling you is the hardest thing to do in these markets. This is why you hear so much about other traders losing so much money: it's because they lose at controlling themselves by not sticking to their objectives and strategies. They're always looking for a better way. There's no better way to win in the market than winning over yourself and your own thinking and perceptions you put on the market. Emotional discipline and risk management will keep you safe in these markets.

Even if your math is as elementary as mine, you too can take profits and stay liquid with thousands of dollars every day without being a math professor.

In the *Way of the Turtle* book and many other trading books, except this one, you will get some new math techniques you may not understand. Don't let that knock you out the game. This book was written to prepare you how to not let that happen.

When I began to study trading—which never stops, by the way...studying, that is—at first, I thought it would be impossible for me to win in this market against all these brilliant minds and their fancy math and machines. Turns out, "brilliant people" need to be brilliant and we need them to be brilliant, but like the little turtles riding on the big turtles' backs, we don't need to know *how* they do it.

In the beginning, when all the math was thrown at me, I thought it was highly possible that I would lose in this game. I must say, though, I have a way of turning losers into winners, and that's just what I have done by applying the philosophy of the "turtle way." The darn thing just resonated with me. I "got it" by simply having the idea to follow the billionaires, millionaires, pension funds, and hedge funds, basically wherever the money goes. And just like the little turtles, I eat where they eat, and so can you. With the internet today, you can follow and track almost anyone or anything. It's like doing detective work.

Nevertheless, these AI's, algos, HFTs, quants, and the hedge funds that use them all have an enormous edge it may seem, but there's still one thing they don't know and are unable to predict unless you yourself tell them. They don't know what you and the billions of participants like you and me are going to do on any given day. It's their life study to one day actually predict what you the at-home hedge fund manager is going to do. That is one of our edges that gives us profitability and keeps on giving it, probably for our lifetime. So, in the beginning, feel the confidence of following the money. How many of you know what "compound interest" is? If you don't, you must pause reading this book and google it. You know I'll wait. Hold me in your lap. #Book

Okay, fine, here's a quick definition: compound interest is interest earned on *principal* plus interest that was earned earlier. You get to double-tap on your cash just for leaving it alone (annually). The finance folks think of compound interest as some kind of magic dust, because it's still one of the most amazing ways left in this country to stack racks and build up your wealth. I enjoy compounding interest and receiving the dividends. (Not only for the money, but because compounding sounds sexy to me.) #BangBang #RIPJohnWitherspoon

So, learn about compound interest and dividends; there's plenty of data out there to guide you on the best stocks that pay the highest yields to their shareholders. Yield is a percentage of more money they add to your investment over a set period of time. Believe it or not, this is where you get paid for hanging out with the corporation of your choice. Your brokerage account will provide you with the tools to discover these businesses. #Easypeazy

A final word about mathematics. I'm so bad at math, I almost can't gamble. I couldn't wrap my head around options, for example, if my life depended on it. I'm too dumb, I think. It sounds fun if you got what homie Jim Cramer calls "mad money" to blow, but I don't have it. I have "funny money," my wallet stays funny. It laughs at me if I even think about gambling in the stock market. It cracks the fu** up, I'm not kiddin' ya!

My money is never at major risk or under pressure. I'm not even a big enough player to be counted by any other big players. All I can tell ya is that the proof is in the pocket, baby. I'm a thousandaire, and I learned how to become a frugal dude. It's not being a cheap dude. Frugal doesn't mean cheap, it means economical and being able to pay your own way. Making economical choices means only buying what I actually need because I can. Adding only products of value that pay me and enjoying the rest. If you're not enjoying your money, you're not doing well. I wish for more people to be doing well.

This book isn't for people who think they're smarter than other people. See, we're not competing with each other; we're sharing, and that creates a whole different vibe. It's a vibe Wall St. isn't that cool with. Wall Street thinks that *sharing is for the snowflakes. You have to be a terror a monster in these markets.* Stop it. No, you don't. You don't have to be insane or a snowflake or any other stupid label public pressure puts on us using the media, podcasts, and blogs. Remember, for them, it's "eat or be eaten," and as far as they're concerned, "dumb money" gets eaten. So be smart. Be Wall Street-Smart. When I was a kid, someone told me "broke" and "poverty" are two separate things. They said when you're broke, nobody helps you (but you); when you're poor, that's when the government s helps you.

· · ·

Now the final, final word. Time is your best friend forever (BFF) in the stock market. No one will support your decision or investment in these volatile markets better than time. In the next book, *Wall Street Game—Game Recognize Game*, I will discuss how on Wall Street, it's not personality that makes you rich, it's knowledge others don't have yet and the disregard for main street. Wall Street has developed into a game because of the evolution of greedy people. They want it all and they want it without you. They don't care if main street partakes in getting paid from the wealth of this country that they live and die for. Up to now main street has been the losers in this game. Every game has losers and winners, it's what makes it a game. Join me in the *Wall Street Game* where we will learn how not to be on the loser's bench but in the winner's pod.

THE END OF THE BEGINNING

SPENCER'S SOURCES

WEBSITES

StockCharts

Investors Hub

TradingView

Seeking Alpha

Market Watch

Small Cap Power

FinViz (stock screener)

Guru Focus

The Fly

Tiingo

Earnings Cast Calls

SOCIAL MEDIA

StockTwits

FinTwit (Twitter)

Instagram

Reddit

Linkedin

Facebook

BOOKS

- Stock Trader's Almanac by Jeffrey A. Hirsch
- A Complete Guide to Volume Price Analysis by Anna Coulling
- Way of the Turtle by Curtis M. Faith
- Market Cycles by Howard Marks
- 100 Best Stocks to Buy in "(current year)" by Peter Sander and Scott Bobo
- Winning the Mental Game on Wall Street by John Magee
- What Works on Wall Street by Jim O'Shaughnessy
- Market Mind Games by Denise Shull
- Big Mistakes by Michael Batnick
- The New Market Wizards by Jack D. Schwager

- Your Money Your Brain by Jason Zweig
- The Little Book that Still Beats the Market by Joel Greenblatt
- An extra author for the list who writes really easy to understand stock market books is Matthew R. Kratter. Check him out on Amazon.

PLEASE LEAVE A REVIEW!

If you have enjoyed getting up on the game, I would be ever so grateful if you could spread the word.

With being a new author, reviews help me gain visibility and they can bring my books to the attention of other potential thousandaires who wish to improve their financial situations.

Leaving a review on Amazon helps others find this book more easily. Thank you in advance. #PayIt-Forward

ABOUT THE AUTHOR

European born actor, **YUL SPENCER,** is a multi-talented performer whose career encompasses television, film, animation, theater, and standup comedy. As a comic, he went by the name of Spencer, toured nationally and has appeared on HBO, Comedy Central and eight seasons on BET's Comic-View. He has acted in hit TV shows like *The Shield and* Malcolm & Eddie, numerous films including *Two Can Play That Game* with Vivica A. Fox and various national commercials.

Yul was inspired for several reasons to write a series of books on the stock market, because many of his colleagues at his age had no "real" money. He was among comedians and actors living a high life because of who they are in the Hollywood industry, but none of them, including himself, had liquid cash or money they had saved. He thought what good is it to be a star at anything and not have access to a minimum of thousands of fu** you dollars.

After contemplating this lifestyle, he wanted to take back control of his finances. Yul wanted to determine how and when money came to him. So, he studied the market for the last ten years and read tons of books and wondered why more regular everyday people aren't investing. Well, what he found out, is that many of the trading books, make things way too complicated and confusing. They're discouraging to the average American. He wanted to write a series of books that offered more encouragement and simplified the way of profiting on the stock market. He felt, if he can do this, anyone can. Though, Yul was born in Europe, he was raised in Oakland, CA. Having been raised in Oakland, Yul has a lot of Street-Smarts, and he has applied his Street-Smarts and Comedy to the Stock Market, because the Stock Market has never been this funny.

These books were written "In response to America's $400.00 Financial crisis." Everyone should have at the very least $400.00 available to them at all times. At his core, Yul believes Americans can put an end to "brokeness" that plagues most citizens. He feels it's time for us all to come up and not let an unexpected $400.00 bill throw us into disarray.

FULL DISCLAIMER

While the author has used his best efforts in preparing this book, he makes no representations or warranties with respect to the accuracy or completeness of the contents of this book and specifically disclaims any implied warranties or merchantability or fitness for a particular purpose. The advice and strategies contained herein may not be suitable for your situation.

You should consult with a legal, financial, tax professional where appropriate. Neither the publisher nor the author shall be liable for any loss of profit or any other commercial damages, including but not limited to special, incidental, consequential, or other damages.

This book is for educational, informational and entertainment purposes only. The views expressed are those of the author alone and should not be taken as expert instruction or commands. The reader is responsible for his or her own actions.

Adherence to all applicable laws and regulations, including international, federal, state, and local laws, is the sole responsibility of the purchaser or reader.

Neither the author nor the publisher assumes any responsibility or liability whatsoever on the behalf of the purchaser or reader of these materials.

Any perceived slight of any individual or organization is purely unintentional.

Past performance is not necessarily indicative of future performance.

Forex, futures, stock and options trading is not appropriate for everyone.

There is a substantial risk of loss associated with trading these markets. Losses can and will occur.

No system or methodology has ever been developed that can guarantee profits of ensure freedom from losses. Nor will it likely ever be.

No representation or implication is being made that using the methodologies or systems or the information contained within this book will generated profits or ensure freedom from losses.

The information contained in this book is for educational, informational and entertainment purposes only and should NOT be taken as investment advice. Examples presented here are not solicitations to buy or sell. The author, publisher, and all affiliates assume no responsibility for your trading results.

THERE IS HIGH RISK IN TRADING!